T0137616

My Testimonies of

Faith and Deliverance

DONNIE RUTH ATKINS-BROWN

authorHOUSE®

AuthorHouse™
1663 Liberty Drive
Bloomington, IN 47403
www.authorhouse.com
Phone: 1 (800) 839-8640

Scripture quotations marked KJV are from the Holy Bible, King James Version (Authorized Version). First published in 1611. Quoted from the KJV Classic Reference Bible, Copyright © 1983 by The Zondervan Corporation.

Published by AuthorHouse 09/23/2016

ISBN: 978-1-5246-4102-3 (sc)
ISBN: 978-1-5246-4101-6 (e)

Library of Congress Control Number: 2016915669

Print information available on the last page.

DEDICATION

This book is dedicated to my amazing daughter,
Reecie Dalsha Holmes, *who I love very much.*
She has inspired me to live a full
life in my senior years,
and has encouraged me to share my testimonies.
My daughters-in-law
Antoinette Sims-Holmes (Ranell)
Sonja Wade-Holmes (Ras)
also
Danielle Eith Brown
Gwen Wiley, too
I love them and I am honored
to call them my daughters.
My nieces
Delois Pippins – Ethel Pippins – Jackie Wiseman
Peggy Miller – Shaun Pippins –Denise Pippins
Lydia Barnes – DeShaune Lockett
Adrienne Wiley – Antaenaeyia Thomas
Rolanda Lane –Karen Lockett – Roxanne Lockett

Contents

Acknowledgements...ix
Foreword..xi
Introduction...xiii

1. GOD – Better Than My Earthly Father.......1
2. Depression - Round One 3
3. Depression - Round Two 5
4. The Hands Of God – part 1.......................7
5. The Hands Of God – part 2.......................9
6. The 5K Race At 67 12
7. Miracles For My children 16
8. A Tough Year...20
9. Everything Belongs to God 25
10. My Birthday...27
11. It's Time To Relocate 29
12. Listen 32
13. Angel In The Airport................................34
14. Vision In A Capsule 36
15. I Have A 24/7 God...................................38
16. What Love Is 40

ACKNOWLEDGEMENTS

I am grateful for my wonderful husband, Phillip whose love, support and understanding has been with me this entire time. That means so much to me. I Love you.

Fred Atkins, my mentor, who shared his experiences with me. He has given me information that I needed and welcomed to complete this book. Thank you.

My Pastor Odell Riley, Power House Church of God in Christ, who prophesied life to me two years ago. He let me know that I have more living to do because the best of my life is yet to come. I am so grateful for my concerned and visionary pastor.

I appreciate and acknowledge Florencetta Gibson, PhD, APMHCNS, and Helen Wiley for their contribution and support.

Last but not least, my deceased parents Deacon Isaac and Mother Olivia Atkins who instilled Christ in our lives. I remember as children, when we could not get to church on Sunday, my parents would call us together on the front porch to teach us the Sunday school lesson. I give glory to God.

FOREWORD

We see people in our everyday lives, nicely dressed, that appear to have everything together. We have no idea of their story. How did they get where they are? What was their childhood like? Were they raised in a two parent home? What challenges have they had to face? What situations have they had to overcome? What failures have they experienced? What successes have they celebrated? Unless they provide some insight, we'll never know. My sister in the Lord, Donnie Brown, has chosen to write this book to provide some insight into her life and her experiences. Through a series of testimonies, she communicates that the Lord has been with her in situations of dire circumstances that appeared hopeless.

Revelation12:10-11 states, "And I heard a loud voice saying in heaven, Now is come salvation, and strength, and the kingdom of our God, and the power of his

Christ: for the accuser of our brethren is cast down, which accused them before our God day and night. And they overcame him be the blood of the Lamb, and by the word of their testimony; and they loved not their lives unto the death." This passage indicates that the combination of the Blood of Jesus and the word of our testimony can assist us in overcoming many of life's challenges. As we communicate our testimonies, we can encourage others to share theirs. We should make the Jesus Christ of the Bible our Savior and be strengthened and encouraged to trust Him in the midst of challenges and circumstances. We will realize that He has provided a path to him and that our journey will bestow glory upon Him.

Thank you, Donnie Brown for sharing your experiences of Highs and lows. Thank you for telling through this series of testimonies about how the Savior was always with you. You validate his word that he will never leave us or forsake us.

Pastor Odell Riley,
Power House Church of God in Christ

INTRODUCTION

Let me tell you this…

I have heard many testimonies of people saying that God had worked a miracle in their lives. He fixed something for them that they had been going through for a long time. They knew it had to be God, but they would not tell exactly what was going on in their lives and what the miracle was about. Our young people need to know the struggles we have gone through before them. They need to know what we have suffered, but we didn't give up on God. They need to know that what they are going through, God has taken others through that same thing.

This book will tell you exactly what I went through, what I did and what God has done for me and through me.

We don't have to let God work it out for us. It is already done; we just need to accept it.

When you read this book you will realize why I wanted to share my **testimonies** with you.

GOD – Better Than My Earthly Father

When I was a small child (the youngest of five children) I would get sleepy in church during the evening worship and walk over to my father to pick me up, and to put me in his lap, so that I could go to sleep. He never pushed me away. I remember him holding me in his arms. Can you imagine how comfortable I felt? Can you imagine how safe I felt? Can you just imagine how loved I felt in my father's arms?

Sometimes there was an altar service. My dad would take me to another adult for them to keep me in their lap so I would be able to continue my sleep, while he was on the altar.

I got up early in the morning to spend time with God in prayer and Bible study. There are times

I would be on the couch feeling God's presence holding me just like a heavenly father would.

Sometimes I think of my earthly father that loved me, but he had to die and leave. My heavenly Father will never leave nor forsake me. God loves me so much more than my father did or could have ever love and care for me.

God's desire is for us to rest in Him. He will take care of all our challenges. Do you realize, He is taking care of our needs when we are asleep, confused and just don't know what to do? He has worked it out already while we are running around trying to make it happen.

> *But God commendeth his love toward*
> *us, in that, . . . Christ died for us.*
> *Romans 5:8 (KJV)*

DEPRESSION - ROUND ONE

For many years I was depressed. Waking up in the morning, all day I was depressed, taking care of my husband, children and the house, until going to bed at night. I took my children to Sunday school and YPWW (Young People Willing Workers) each Sunday night and Bible Band during the week. I don't remember how many years this cycle continued. I don't know why I just didn't get it. So many times I felt like just giving up.

The depression would get worse in the beginning of November and would not get any better until well into the next year.

The children and I would take a nap every day after lunch. This particular day Satan had already begun to talk to me about ending it all. You don't have to put up with this; just kill yourself while the children are asleep. Then I thought of my children; who would love them, care for them, and raise them like I would? Then Satan said "Why not just kill yourself and your children? That would clear up everything.

I waited until they fell asleep. I then went to the gas stove and turned on all four eyes on the stove and the oven and was about to lay down with them so we could just sleep away together. I just did not want them to suffer like I had suffered; I could not bear the thought of it. Then the spirit of God spoke to me "Your children deserve a chance to live." He only had to say it one time, because He knew I loved them so much and wanted them to have a good life. I got up opened the windows and doors to let the gas out and I later lay down with them and had a good nap. After this, I began a life of prayer and started to read my Bible for myself and asked God to open the scriptures up to me.

DEPRESSION - ROUND TWO

But Satan was not finished with me yet, that was just a little hurdle to begin my deliverance.

After a while I got enough of it. One day my children were not home, nobody was in the house except for me. I began to pray and asked God to manifest Himself in me "today." The spirit of God begins to rise up in me. I told the devil "I have enough of your evil spirit; you have to get out of this house." I began at the rear of the house, walked through each room, casting him out of my house. I opened each cabinet, each door in the bedrooms, under the beds, in the bathrooms, the kitchen, the laundry room, the living room, the dining room, the hallway, and the den. I even opened the windows and the front door and told him to get out in the name of JESUS. I have been in church all my life, hearing the saints rebuking the devil and casting him out. Now it is actually real to me. Satan was demanded to get out of my house and don't come back (the blood of Jesus has been applied). I am sure some of the neighbors must have heard me, but that didn't matter to me. Trust me, I was speaking loud and clear. He had to go; there was no space for him anymore in this house.

After getting Satan out, I was so tired, but this was the best tiredness I have ever experienced before or since.

Would you believe I was free from that depressed feeling? My soul, my body, my mind, my life was all free. I started to feel light. I started to see free, I started to walk free. I started to think free. I started to feel free. I was FREE. The pain and burden that Satan had on me was gone. When my children returned home from school they noticed the difference; I was not staying in bed all the time. When I went to church the members noticed the change in me.

God does not want us depressed, sick, or feeling sorry for ourselves. He wants us to be free.

Submit yourselves therefore to God. Resist the devil and he will flee from you. James 4:7 (KJV)

THE HANDS OF GOD – part 1

My family and I were just beginning our dream vacation of a lifetime, which I had planned well. We were so excited about all the states we were going to visit, places we had never been before.

Shortly after leaving Los Angeles, we witnessed an accident (after it had happened). It was a truck with a camper that had turned over in a deep ditch. We could not tell if anyone was seriously hurt or killed. The way the accident appeared, their belongings were scattered all over, even the camper had separated from the truck. That frightened me so much that I began to pray for God's protection over us and our vehicle. Then I remembered the request for prayer I made to my pastor and the church before we left. I felt at ease, comfortable, and protected that everything would go well.

As we continued our trip, I was looking out the window and I saw a vision of a large hand, the length of our vehicle. I looked on the other side there was another one. I didn't have to ask, I knew they were the hands of God.

We travelled through twenty states that summer with absolutely no problems. When there were accidents on the highway, I would feel uncomfortable, and then I would immediately think of the hands of God with us, and pray for the people that were involved. That was our best trip ever!

THE HANDS OF
GOD – part 2

Thirty five years later, I was traveling with my grandchildren, Loren and Sydney, who visited me for summer vacation. We left from Dallas to return them to their parents in Los Angeles. Our flight was scheduled for no changes, but to stop in El Paso to allow passengers to get off and new passengers to get on then continue our flight into Los Angeles. After the new passengers were on the plane, we were headed to Los Angeles. As we began to taxi on the runway, the plane begins to pick up speed. I noticed something different about this so I said to myself "This must be a new pilot." The plane continued on to full speed and suddenly it stopped. I noticed most of the passengers were frightened. We waited for a long time for someone to tell us what had happened, and why we had to stop. But they waited; it seemed like about 20 minutes before they made the announcement that something was wrong with the plane. Finally, they said that a mechanic will come to the plane on the runway and repair it, and then we will be on our way. We must have waited another 30 minutes before the flight attendant told us the plane could not be repaired there on the runway. We will have to return to the airport for the repairs to be done there, and it will not take very long, we will be on our way shortly. The plane was towed back for the repairs. While we waited for a half hour or longer, the captain spoke to us and told us the engine had **blown out.** The plane cannot be repaired here. All of the passengers had to get off and finish the trip on another plane.

After getting on a different plane, I was sitting there looking out of the window and saw, again, the vision of God's hand beside the plane. I smiled, closed my eyes, and whispered a praise of thanks. Then a soothing voice spoke in my spirit "These hands have never left you." Oh, how I praised God that day sitting on that airplane all the way to Los Angeles. I felt like I couldn't wait to share this with my family. They know that I have visions of this nature. I am grateful for their faith to believe me.

Sometimes I think that Satan has tried to destroy me before this incident, but the hands of God did not allow that. I can say without a doubt that God is everywhere all the time. This has been proven to me over and over again.

..I will never leave thee, nor forsake thee. Hebrew 13:5 (KJV)

The 5K Race At 67

In previous years my daughter would run and I walked in 5k races with no problem sometime twice a month. We've and have won some of the races. But now I am older and haven't walked that distance for four or five years. So I decided to give it a try. I wanted to walk in the *Norma Lampert 5k race and walk for Lupus in Little Rock, AR.* I began to self-train by walking around Walmart's parking lot, and when the weather was not favorable I would walk inside. I enjoyed the training. I felt this would be a life lesson for me and something I could share with my young adult Sunday school class.

A few days before the race, something happened to the car. The mechanic said the car could not be repaired in time for us to get to Little Rock for the race. My husband was uncomfortable and did not want to take that chance. I told him to please let's go, I have to be in that race. We made it to Little Rock with very little problems.

The day of the race, both my husband and I were excited. While waiting at the starter line I thought there would be a burst of energy to get me going when the gun fired to start the race. The gun fired; there was no burst of energy for me. The other contestants start walking, running, laughing and talking, they all seemed so happy. I decided to just take my time and not rush. No matter how many passed me it was ok. I just continued to take my time and walk. No one was walking with me so it was easy to keep my mind on the Lord.

As the walk continued, I fell further and further behind, but I was still encouraged to continue. My mind, my heart, my spirit, all of me was at peace. The hills were hard to climb. Each one was tougher than the last one, but my mind was on the finish line. As the race continued there were no contestants in sight. The volunteers had taken up the cones and chairs and left their posts.

From seemingly nowhere a lady joined me, and began to walk with me; she was not a contestant. Her company was strength for me.

As we walked and talked I began to feel better and stronger. Shortly after, sheriffs on horses joined us and followed us closely. One of them said to me that I don't have to continue if I didn't feel like it. A pickup came next to me going very slowly, the driver told me to get on the truck if I can't make it. Oh, how I wanted to get on the bed of that truck and just lie down. I replied no thanks; I want to get to the finish line by walking.

Every time I would feel like giving up, the finish line would come before my eyes. I knew I had to make it there by walking. We came to a large hill, the largest one in the path. I was ready to give up and just stop walking right there. The lady with me said the finish line is right on the other side of that hill and pass the curve. I was exhausted, but I kept walking. She said you don't have far to go. After going over that hill, I looked up and there was another small hill in the curve. I kept walking. When I reached the top of the small hill, she pointed and said "there's the finish line." I wanted to just take off and run! I tried to lift my feet to run, but I couldn't. My legs and feet were just too heavy.

As I walked closer to where I thought was the finish line, it was something else. Oh-My-God, how disappointed I was. I had to walk another .1 mile to get there. When I reached the finish line, what a great feeling of accomplishment I had. The sheriffs on their horses were right there with me as I crossed the finish line. I don't know what happened to the young lady that walked and talked with me. But I do know God sent me the help I needed for that race. God gave me strength, and the mind to continue and not give up. It is good that God loves us all. He did that for me, He will do it for you in any situation.

Two weeks later I received a trophy in the mail for 2nd place to finish in my age group.

...the race is not to the swift, nor
the battle to the strong...
Ecclesiastes 9:11 (KJV)

MIRACLES FOR
MY CHILDREN

My daughter

Before my children began to attend school I would make some of their clothes. I remember making the three of them overcoats. The boys' coats were brown velvet, fully lined and my daughter's coat was royal blue, fully lined and trimmed with white fur. The coat was very beautiful and she loved it. She wanted to wear it all the time, even around in the house.

One wash day I got up early and washed a load of clothes when they had finished washing, I checked on the children to make sure they were asleep before leaving to go outside to hang them up. The children were all asleep in their beds. I left quietly to go out without disturbing them. It took me less than fifteen minutes to finish the clothes and return back into the house. When I walked in the house I immediately checked on the children. My daughter was not in her bed. I called her and looked through the house, but she was nowhere to be found. Where can my child be? So I did what any mother would do – I panicked. Then I went outside calling for her; checked the neighbors houses, no one was home. I started running up the street toward the busy corner of the street. I saw a neighbor from across the street walking toward me with something in her arms. I cried out and asked her has she seen my baby. She said softly, "Here she is right here." My neighbor had my daughter in her arms and I did not recognize her, I was blind with fear. My neighbor said my daughter was in that busy street. She had on her new royal blue coat that I made for her.

She had woken up, gotten out of bed, took her coat out of the closet and put it on, then walked out of the house without making any noise. I am sure she was looking for me.

God was watching over her.

My first son

My second child and oldest son was ten years old, playing in a neighbor's yard and fell on a broken bottle and made a severe, very deep cut in his leg. The blood was flowing out very badly. I wrapped his leg in a large bath towel and rushed him to the emergency room. I was so afraid and thinking maybe small pieces of glass would get lost in the wound. As we were going to the hospital, he never cried, but watched me. He knew I was very upset. My son was calm as if nothing had happened. When we got to the emergency room it did not take long for the doctor to see him. The doctor took the towel off of his leg. What I saw, I couldn't believe my eyes. The cut had stopped bleeding, and the doctor proceeded to dress his wound. I don't remember how many stiches it took, but it was a lot.

While riding home, he told me the reason his leg had stopped bleeding was because he prayed and ask God to stop it from bleeding, and He did. It was good to know my child had that kind of faith in God. God hears the innocent prayers of children. HALLELUJAH!!

The youngest child

My youngest son was attending college. One day he forgot to get money for gas to put in his car, so he decided to go as far as his car could on the gas he had already. On his way, he had to stop at a traffic light that was close to a bus stop. There was a lady standing there that had missed the bus. She needed to get to work on time. She opened the car door of my son's car and got in. Then she told him to go to the bus stop ahead of the bus so she could catch it; and he did. As she was getting out of the car she put money on the seat and got out. She left him enough money to get gas for the car and buy his lunch for that day. God is so good!

The eyes of the Lord are in everyplace...
Proverb15:3 (KJV)

A TOUGH YEAR

I had been suffering with female problems for years, but now the symptoms began to get worse. I made an appointment to see my doctor to find out what was going on in this body of mine.

The doctor examined me, and then invited me into his office to give me information on what he had just found in the examination. He told me that I had fibroid tumors in my uterus, but there is nothing to worry about. He continued and said you are close to menopause now they may dissolve, but we will keep an eye on them and come back next month. (This was in February)

I kept my appointment for that next month (March). This time he told me the tumors were growing, but let's wait another month to be sure.

I returned to the doctor's office in April. Now I could feel the tumors in my uterus by rubbing my stomach; I knew then I was in trouble. After the exam this time, he said to me the tumors were growing faster than a fetus, and he would have to make arrangements for you to have emergency surgery.

Before I could have surgery, my sister suddenly passed away. How horrifying that was for me.

So now, Satan had new assignments: to frighten me, to make me lose faith in God, and to just give up. He told me I was going to die on the operating table. I would go to sleep and have dreams of dying, and wake up with an anxiety attack. They would come without warning; even while driving on the Los Angeles freeways, or just sitting talking, anytime it felt like it they would come and I would feel like each breath would be my last one, but I would never stop praying. I knew God had a word for me. I searched the scriptures to find something that was printed in red that Jesus had spoken. I could not find anything that was satisfying.

One day I picked up the Bible to read and the Bible just fell open to Isaiah chapter 41. I began to read starting at the beginning of the chapter and read through to the tenth verse. I yelled "This is what I need." Jesus spoke to me through this verse: *"Fear thou not; for I am with thee: be not dismayed; for I am thy God: I will strengthen thee; yea, I will help thee; yea, I will uphold thee with the right hand of my righteousness." Isaiah 41:10 (KJV).* After reading this verse I was strengthened. When that fear would come on me, I would read it over and over again, until I memorized it. That is a Satan fleeing scripture.

Time had come for me to be admitted into the hospital for surgery. There was no fear, no anxiety, just the peace of God. I knew all was well, when I saw an angel of God appears standing at the foot of my bed while I was being prepped for surgery.

The nurse came to me to give me a shot. I asked her why and what it's for? She said it is to keep me calm. I told her I did not need it because I was already calm.

My recovery from that surgery was quick and without any problems. Before being discharged, I went visiting people on that floor that was ill and I was able to encourage them.

The day I was discharged, my daughter picked me up from the hospital. As we were on our way home, I asked how the boys and the house were. She said the boys and the house were fine, but they were at home alone, except for one night. I remember the person promised me they would be there with my children. Something happened to me inside. The respect, honor, and all trust left me at that moment for that person. I was not hurt or disappointed: I felt I already knew it would happen; I was not surprised about it.

Shortly after I came home, I received a letter from my employer stated that my job was closed. That meant when I am well enough to return to work there will be no job for me, and I should look for other employment. There I was alone with my three children, my daughter was in college, my two sons were in high school, and the oldest one was going into his senior year. Now all the responsibility was for me to take - the house payments, clothes, food and utilities.

There were times when I felt there was no way out. There were sleepless nights, wet pillows, walking the floor and more bills than money. I can't say I held on to God, because He held me and carried me through. I am so glad He did because I was not strong enough to hold on. During that time my heart was so heavy; it felt like God had forgotten me, and nobody else cared. There were times I fell on my face to the floor, crying "God help me, why am I going through this? I don't deserve this!

I have heard ministers say repeatedly "God got your back," but now I know that God not only has my back, but He has all of me in His hands. If only my back is covered what will happen to my front, and sides and the rest of me?

Casting all of your care upon him; for He
careth for you. 1Peter 5:7(KJV)

EVERYTHING BELONGS TO GOD

The children had gone to bed for the night, I was relaxing, watching television, enjoying the moment of being alone at the end of another completely exhausting the day. Then there was cracking in the hallway with the sound of footsteps. I looked and saw flashing lights. I got up to see what was going on. Can you believe the rear of my house was on fire? I got the children out of bed, gathered them and took them outside.

Neighbors came over to help me get the furniture out of the house. I don't know who called 911, it could have been me, or one of the neighbors, I don't know. The fire department put the fire out and placed plastic over the windows and told me it is safe enough for us to stay. The fire completely destroyed the garage and severely damaged one of the bedrooms. The chief fireman told me that someone had set the fire in the back of our garage.

A few days after the fire, I was looking out of the kitchen window at the damage and feeling bad over what had just happened. Then I began to thank God for taking care of us.

A song began to come out of my mouth, from my soul "All that I have belongs to the Lord," I have nothing no not I He let me use them for just a little while. The song continues, this house that I am living in belong to the Lord, all of my children belongs to the Lord. The clothes that we are wearing belong to the Lord. In other word, everything belongs to the Lord.

The earth and everything in it, the
world and its inhabitants,
Belong to the Lord. Psalm 24:1 (KJV)

MY BIRTHDAY

Growing up in Northeast Louisiana, Morehouse Parish, we were very poor, the poorest family in the community. But I had dreams of having a birthday party and I wanted to travel all over the United States and beyond. When December would get close I would get excited, because I thought this would be the year that my parents would give me a birthday party. I would make my invitations, take my mother's envelopes and put them inside so I could mail them to my cousins and friends. I was so disappointed when Mama told me there will be no party this year. So I would ask for a gift for my birthday, I didn't get that either. They would tell me to wait until Christmas, which is two weeks after. Then for Christmas, I would get the same thing everyone else got-two apples and two oranges. This went on year after year. I did not realize that we were so poor.

My sister Helen's birthday is on Valentine Day, it seems she always got gifts but I didn't get any for my birthday. I couldn't understand that.

I was twenty five when I was given my first party; it was a small group of church people. The guests were generous and enjoyable. My husband wanted to surprise me, but didn't know how; that was funny.

Years went by, but the desire to have *the party* never left me. For my fiftieth birthday I gave myself a party at my house and later went on a cruise. After that I went every year for the next ten years to celebrate. There were, also, other cruises I went on for vacations and to celebrate other birthdays during those years.

IT'S TIME TO RELOCATE

The children had grown up, one was married and the other two were in college and working. I felt in my spirit it was time to move to another location. But Lord, I had put too much money in that house redecorating to sell it now. I will not be able to get out of it what was just put in it. I had become very uncomfortable in this house. There was no more enjoyment in there for me; I agreed with my spirit to put the house on the market.

The house was on the market for nearly a year without an offer. No one had even come to view it. It is time now to talk to God about this ordeal; what was I going to do? It was time for God to take over; He knows what to do.

I had to attend a meeting with the Juvenile Hall Ministry one Saturday afternoon. On my way to the meeting, I was driving on the freeway with my mind on the house and praying and wondering what was I going to do? I remembered the scripture: So, what I had to do was speak to that house and tell it to get off the market. My mind was made up at that moment, when I got home that was exactly what I would do.

I went to the meeting, but don't remember what happened. My mind was on casting that house off the market and nothing else.

Coming home I began to think; I will have to speak to this house. How am I going to do that without embarrassing myself? The neighbors will be watching me and telling the others neighbors, that didn't see it. "She has just lost her mind. She was in front of her house talking to it and waving her hands."

When I got to the house, parked my car, got out and walked to the front and began to talk to it with a voice loud enough for the house to hear me, saying "House get off the market, you are sold, you must go, in Jesus name." There was no embarrassment at all; I was just obeying God's word.

Later that evening a woman came by to see the house, it was encouraging to me to think somebody is interested.

Monday the realtor called me for an appointment. Someone was interested in my house – WOW. He brought someone over to look at the house that evening.

He called me again Tuesday and said there was another family that was interested and wants to see the house. They came to see it.

The family that sent a representative on Monday to see the house called the realtor on Wednesday and said the whole family wanted to see it. They came that evening to inspect it. After they left that evening, the realtor called me back and told me that family wanted my house and would pay my asking price for it.

Thank you Lord!!! NOW THAT'S ANOTHER WAY GOD WORKS!

> *For verily I say unto you, that whosoever shall say unto this mountain, Be thou removed, and be thou cast into the sea; and shall not doubt in his heart, but shall believe that those things which he saith shall come to pass; he shall have whatsoever he saith. St. Mark 11:23 (KJV).*

LISTEN

There have been many women, including my mother, who has passed on, but deposited nuggets in my life. I have maintained those words of advice and encouragement and will not let go of them.

One day at work, an older woman and I were talking about how the children during that time were so disobedient and ungrateful. She proceeded to tell me that if I keep my children in church and be sure they are active in church activities for their age group; I will not have to worry about them. They will stay away from trouble, grow up loving God and will serve Him. And that would make me proud.

That teaching will not leave them; they will remember and live by it for the rest of their lives.

I made a vow to God that day (and kept it) that I would do just that!

My children have grown up to be adults and I am not ashamed of them. They love God and are serving Him. Would you believe my oldest son has been called to be a minister? He is anointed to preach the gospel of Christ. When he was two years old he was preaching in diapers. The only word we could understand him to say was "JESUS."

It is good to listen to seniors, because they have the experience.

Train up a child in the way he should go: and when he is old, he will not depart from it. Proverb 22:6 (KJV)

ANGEL IN THE AIRPORT

After the women's convention in Denver, Colorado I planned to go to Los Angeles to attend my son's graduation that afternoon. The courtesy car took me to the airport. Because of my eye problem from laser surgery, I was unable to focus at distances; this made me uncomfortable to be alone in a strange place.

I walked in this large airport, looked around, panicked, and dropped my carry-on to the floor then said to myself, what am I going to do if no one is here to assist me? A lady dressed in white appeared standing next to me. She asked me, "You were here for the women's convention, huh?" I replied "yes, I was, but I don't know where to go from here." I was so confused. People were all over the airport, it seemed there was no organization in that place at all. I told her about my eye problem and the airline I was travelling on. She said she would show me how to get to where I needed to go.

She stayed with me through security and baggage check. As we began to walk through the corridor toward the waiting areas, she pointed out there is your airline waiting area, but I could not see it. We walked a few steps farther and she pointed again and said "you wait for your plane right there." At that time I could see it. I said, "Thanks very much." She had been so good to me I had decided to buy lunch for her. I opened my mouth to tell her, but she was gone. I turned completely around but she was nowhere to be found.

Be not forgetful to entertain strangers;
for thereby some have entertained angels
unawares. Hebrews 13:2 (KJV)

VISION IN A CAPSULE

Approximately five years ago I began to see a vision of me sitting in an object like a capsule, hanging in midair, about twelve inches above the ground. The weather was overcast. I could see children playing in the streets; adults were going to and fro taking care of their business. Everything seemed normal.

As I sat in the capsule, I observed the environment it was clear to me; I could see and understand everything that was going on around me, but they didn't see me. It was just as if I was not there. I could tell I was not of this world.

As each day passed the capsule, with me still in it would rise higher and higher until it reached the clouds. As I entered the cloud it was light and as I rose higher into the cloud it would get darker and darker until I could see nothing, not even my hands before me. I was in the dark cloud for two days.

Two weeks later the vision came back to me and continued. Now I was out of the capsule and standing on the edge of a very high cliff. The sun was shining, it was clear, not a cloud in the sky. I looked down below me. There was a prairie with acres and acres of grass and small patches of weeds that were half dead. In the center of this prairie was a huge patch of high bushes or small trees. Much like the grass, they were near dead.

Days later the vision returned and continued, there I was still standing on the edge of this cliff, I had the urge to jump off, but I refused.

One week later the prairie rose up to the level of the cliff, but didn't connect right away. It later connected, but the prairie was all green. I stepped to get on the prairie grass, the vision ended.

This vision lasted for more than a month.

I HAVE A 24/7 GOD

No, I can never say "God got my back." What would happen to the front of me, to the sides of me, to the top of me and to the bottom of me, if He only has my back?

My God is carrying me safely, comfortably while I rest completely protected in His arms. I don't know what He is going to do with me. I don't know where He is carrying me. I don't know what He will take me through. My trust is in Him to take me where He wants me to go and to do what He wants me to do.

There have been tough times when I felt like there was no way out. There have been more bills than money. There have been sleepless nights and wet pillows, because I was not trusting God.

My desire is not to dwell on the negative, because God has more grace and deliverance that I could ever have problems.

I am writing this little book to glorify and magnify God and God alone, and to let you know or to just remind you that God is a **24/7 God**.

WHAT LOVE IS

We say *I love you* to many people; family members, friends, coworkers, peers, fellow church members and sometimes strangers. Do we really love them? Love is not love unless it is shared.

Where there is love, there is giving of oneself, time, money, and words that express concern for their well-being. Love will rejoice with you and when you are sad love is sad with you.

Love is not hidden. Love is not waiting and definitely not expecting anything, but love in return. If there is no return, love will continue to give anyway.

For God so loved the world, that He
gave His only begotten son.
St. John 3:16a (KJV)

GOD BLESS YOU

The Lord bless thee, and keep thee:

The Lord make his face shine upon thee,

and be gracious unto thee:

The Lord lift up his countenance upon thee,

and give thee peace.

(Numbers 6: 24-26 KJV)

Printed in the United States
By Bookmasters